THE OFFICIAL
Elvis Presley
FAN CLUB

COMMEMORATIVE
ALBUM

THE OFFICIAL
Elvis Presley
FAN CLUB

COMMEMORATIVE
ALBUM
1935 – 1977

First published in Great Britain in 1997 by
Virgin Books
an imprint of Virgin Publishing Ltd
332 Ladbroke Grove
London W10 5AH

A catalogue record for this book is available from the British Library.

ISBN 1-85227 629 0

Designed by Blackjacks, London
Reproduction and photo retouching by Scanners.

Printed and bound in Great Britain by
Jarrold Book Printing, Thetford, Norfolk

Introduction

All Shook Up

*e*lvis made his first appearance in the UK chart in May 1956. His first gold record *Heartbreak Hotel* started it all. It paved the way for popular music today and started a fan phenomena, unrivalled by any other artist.

The Official Elvis Presley Fan Club of Great Britain was established in August 1957 when Elvis was enjoying chart success with his first UK No.1 single *All Shook Up*. Originally founded in London's Mayfair by Jeanne Saword and Dug Surtees the club cost the equivalent of 55p to join, for which members received five bi-monthly magazines, two journals and free glossy black and white photographs.

The Official Elvis Presley Fan Club of Great Britain and the Commonwealth was first registered with the British Board of Trade in 1957 and was re-registered by Albert Hand Publications Limited in 1961. Albert Hand had been publisher of the hugely successful *Elvis Monthly* since 1960 and when Dug and Jeanne went their own way in early 1962, Albert took over as Fan Club Secretary. The new publication was entitled *Elvis Express* and membership was the equivalent of a mere 27½p. The fan club was the first official fan club outside of the USA which enjoyed the blessing of Elvis and the Colonel and in 1967 the club was re-assigned to its new Secretary Todd Slaughter, again with official endorsement.

Todd Slaughter excelled in his role as Fan Club Secretary for 28 years. In 1972 the club began organising trips to the United States so that fans could see, and a lucky few meet, their idol. Todd's outstanding work with the media earned the club recognition world-wide, building its fan-base to one of Elvis' largest. In November 1994 Todd underwent heart transplant surgery and although making an excellent recovery resigned as club secretary in December 1995.

Stepping into the role of Fan Club Secretary was not easy. I didn't really know who Elvis was until his untimely death in August 1977, when I was only eight. In the years that followed, Elvis films were prime time television viewing, captivating a whole new generation of fans, including myself. This still continues today as people turn away from contemporary music in the nineties and go back to the origins of popular music. Backed with our original members and future generations of fans, the Official Elvis Presley Fan Club continues to live up to its reputation as the most respected fan organisation in the world.

Julie Mundy

The 1950s

"I Don't Sound Like Nobody"

*i*t was the summer of '53 when nineteen-year-old Elvis Presley called into the Memphis Recording Service at 706 Union Avenue to record *My Happiness*, reportedly a gift for his mother. The Memphis Recording Service was home of the Sun Record label, owned by Sam Phillips, and on this historical day, in his absence, the recording was handled by his assistant Marion Keisker. When Marion questioned Elvis on whom he sounded like, his response was simple; "I don't sound like nobody."

During the session, Marion was so impressed by this young singer that she kept a recording to play for Sam on his return. Elvis, however, didn't meet Sam Phillips until January 1954, when he returned to record a second disc. Like Marion, Sam was impressed by the young singer and the following summer called Elvis into the studio to record the song *Without You*. Elvis was teamed with musicians Scotty Moore and Bill Black for the recording. Although the session was unsuccessful, the liaison proved promising and on July 5th Elvis, Scotty and Bill recorded Arthur "Big Boy" Crudup's *That's All Right*.

Given its first radio airplay the following week, the song was an immediate hit locally and before long Elvis was the fastest rising star in the region. Elvis, Scotty and Bill, or The Blue Moon Boys as they were known were soon touring regularly throughout the south. In October 1954 their appearance on the live Saturday night country music radio show *The Louisiana Hayride* resulted in exposure on 190 radio stations networked throughout thirteen states. A year's contract, as well as countless new engagements soon followed.

Already attracting attention from America's teenage population, Elvis had also caught the attention of promoter Colonel Tom Parker and in August 1955 signed a management contract with Colonel Parker and Hank Snow Attractions. A unique partnership that continued throughout Elvis' lifetime and remains legendary to this day.

In November 1955 the Colonel and RCA successfully negotiated a deal to buy Elvis' recording contract from Sun Records, for an unprecedented $40,000, with Elvis receiving a bonus of $5,000. Elvis' Sun recordings were immediately re-released making him a national star, and in January 1956, the release of *Heartbreak Hotel*, from his first recording session at RCA, turned the twenty-one-year-old into an international sensation.

Elvis with Bob Neal, his manager prior to Colonel Parker and Sam Phillips, owner of the Sun record label

Elvis surrounded by fans in Lubbock, Texas, where he appeared with the Blue Moon Boys whilst touring the southern states in 1956. On the far right is a promising young local singer, Buddy Holly

April 15th 1956, in an RCA recording studio receiving his first gold disc
for his first RCA release, Heartbreak Hotel

*Elvis' second appearance on the Milton Berle show on June 5th created a
national outcry following his provocative performance of Hound Dog.
Around the same time, he had a run-in with a Memphis traffic cop.
Elvis hammed it up for the photographer and the entire incident was
far less confrontational than it looks here*

Despite his phenomenal success with the nation's teenagers, his first
Las Vegas appearance at the Frontier Hotel in April/May 1956
received only a lukewarm response from the adult audience

April 6th 1956, following a screen test on the 1st, Elvis signs a seven year movie contract with Hal Wallis and Paramount Pictures

June 20th 1956. Having fun after his appearance on local Memphis TV show Wink Martindale's Dance Party

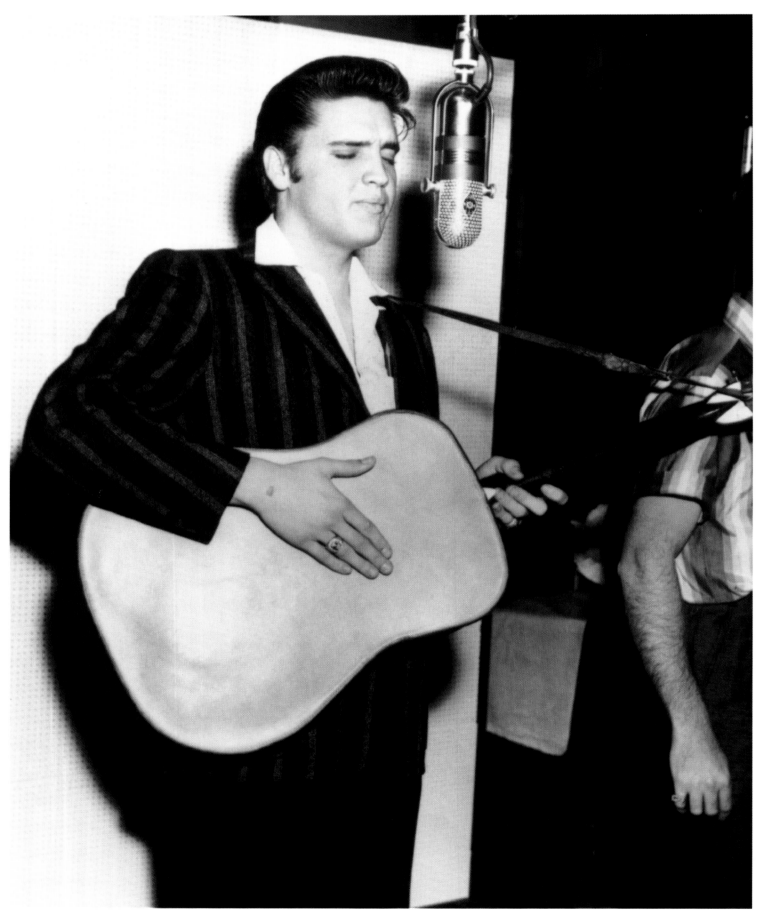

July 2nd 1956, at RCA recording Don't Be Cruel

*Although contracted to Paramount Pictures, Elvis, pictured here on set
with co-star Debra Paget, was loaned to 20th Century Fox for his
first feature film* Love Me Tender

Signing autographs for fans on location for Love Me Tender

In Love Me Tender
Elvis played Clint Reno

*Elvis pictured on location
for* Love Me Tender

Originally titled The Reno Brothers *Elvis' first movie was renamed*
Love Me Tender *to take advantage of the success of the end theme,*
which had been released as a single

*At the age of 21 when he embarked on his movie career, Elvis wanted to
become a serious actor, and follow in the footsteps of James Dean and
Marlon Brando, whom he had always admired*

*A candid shot taken on the sound-stage during
production of* Love Me Tender

July 4th 1956. On stage at Russwood Park, Memphis, during an early performance with his backing singers, the Jordanaires, who continued to back Elvis throughout his movie career

Elvis during a session at Radio Recorders in Hollywood, September 1956

*A publicity shot from 1956. Already developing a taste for fine jewelry, Elvis
is pictured wearing his famous horseshoe ring. Designed by Harry Levitch,
Elvis gave many copies of this ring away as gifts to friends and family*

September 26th 1956. Elvis Presley Day is proclaimed in his birthtown, Tupelo, Mississippi. Elvis performed two shows at the Mississippi, Alabama Fair and Dairy Show, the same venue that he made his first public performance at the age of ten, singing Old Shep

Posing for cameras at the Mississippi Alabama Fair and Dairy Show

Elvis during the first of three appearances on Toast of The Town
hosted by Ed Sullivan. September 9th 1956

In rehearsal and in performance on September 9th for the show that, at the time, attracted the highest ever ratings for a variety show

Greeting the fans while filming the Ed Sullivan show on September 9th

*October 28th 1956. Elvis and Ed Sullivan, during rehearsals for his
second appearance on* Toast of The Town

Publicity shot for Elvis' second movie Loving You. Paramount *1957*

After singing Teddy Bear *in* Loving You *fans responded by sending thousands of teddys to Elvis*

Loving You *was Elvis' first colour feature film*

Performing Lonesome Cowboy *as the rising singing star*
Deke Rivers in Loving You

On Stage with the Jordanaires in Loving You

Elvis with co-star 'Lizabeth Scott during production of Loving You

10212-109

Loving You *was specially written for Elvis, with the rise to fame of Elvis'*
character Deke Rivers supposedly mirroring Elvis' own career

Elvis meeting fans during production of Loving You *on his 'Hound Dog' bicycle, presented to him by the studio. The guitar plaque below the crossbar bears the legend 'Hound Dog'*

Elvis purchased Graceland in March 1957 for $100,000 and is pictured here meeting fans from behind the legendary music gates that he had installed at the mansion

39

The 1950s – "I Don't Sound Like Nobody"

Elvis in his gold lamé suit as designed by Nudie of Hollywood. The suit was made of a high polished leather and due to its weight Elvis tended to wear the jacket only

March 28th 1957. At a press conference before an appearance in Chicago

*Elvis receiving an award for Top Artist in a popularity poll
in Ottawa, Canada, in 1957. Elvis' Canadian dates that year represented
the only performances he ever gave outside of the United States*

April 5th 1957. Performing at the Sports Arena in Philadelphia

October 28th 1957. Performing at the Pan Pacific Auditorium Los Angeles.
By now the gold lamé trousers were rarely seen

A pensive shot of Elvis taken in 1957. By now his fame had spread
worldwide, even to the closed countries of the former Eastern Bloc in Europe
where bootleg Elvis recordings were made on discarded X-ray plates

May 1957. A wardrobe still for his third movie, Jailhouse Rock, *with his third film studio, MGM. The name of the previous actor to appear on this particular wardrobe blackboard was Yul Brynner*

As Vince Everett in Jailhouse Rock

Many of Elvis' friends, fellow musicians, songwriters and family members appeared as extras throughout his movie career. Pictured in this scene from Jailhouse Rock *are musicians Bill Black and DJ Fontana, songwriter Mike Stoller, cousin Junior Smith, disc jockey George Klein, and founder member of the Memphis Mafia, Lamar Fike*

Recording the soundtrack for Jailhouse Rock *at Radio Recorders, California with original Blue Moon Boys, Bill Black on Elvis' left and Scotty Moore, far right*

With cell mate Hunk Houghton (Mickey Shaughnessy) in Jailhouse Rock

September 1957. At a press conference whilst appearing in Portland, Oregon

Publicity shot for Elvis' fourth movie King Creole, *Paramount 1958*

10216-78

Based on the Harold Robbins novel A Stone For Danny Fisher, *and
directed by Michael Curtiz (famed for* Casablanca*).* King Creole *is
regarded as Elvis' greatest acting performance*

A candid shot taken during production of King Creole

Elvis with Walter Matthau as the underground boss Maxie Fields in King Creole

Elvis stops to sign autographs in Jackson Square, New Orleans,
on location for King Creole

Elvis as Danny Fisher singing Lover Doll. *In the original novel, the main character, Danny Fisher, was a boxer, but this was changed to the role of a singer in the screenplay*

With co-star Carolyn Jones in King Creole

*After receiving a draft
notice the previous
Christmas, Elvis was
given a deferment in
order to complete* King
Creole, *but to his fans'
dismay was inducted
into the U.S. Army in
March 1958*

*At Graceland, June 1958,
Elvis with his father
Vernon Presley during his
first army leave*

This shot was taken during a recording session in Nashville in June 1958
while Elvis was on leave from the army

Private U.S.55330761 enjoys the attentions of fan Gloria Mowels whilst stationed in Texas during his basic training

Elvis sailed from New York aboard the U.S.S. Randall, arriving in West Germany on October 1st 1958

Elvis' arrival in Germany was a well orchestrated army P.R. affair, but once the fuss died down, he was joined by his father, grandmother and close friends. Nevertheless he was still suffering from the loss of his mother Gladys who had died two months earlier

Living in a rented house in Bad Neuheim, Elvis would spend time meeting fans who visited his residence daily

*December 26th 1958. Elvis visiting the 'Holiday on Ice' show
while on leave in Frankfurt*

Meeting Swedish rock-n-roll singer Little Gerhard

Elvis didn't receive any special privileges while serving in the army. He completed his service as a regular solder

Three months after being promoted to Sergeant, Elvis left Germany on March 1st 1960 and was officially discharged from duty on March 5th

The 1960s

"Tired of Singing to the Guys I Beat Up in the Movies"

*a*fter two years away in the army Elvis was concerned that his absence may have damaged his career. He didn't need to worry, his fans followed him home in their thousands and back in Memphis, the world's media were beating down his door.

Elvis' first post-army recording session took place in Nashville in March 1960 and he returned to the UK charts the following month with *Stuck on You*, which was followed by further successes with *The Girl of My Best Friend* and later in the year by the No.1 single *It's Now Or Never*. Following this recording session Elvis taped *Welcome Home, Elvis*, a special edition of Frank Sinatra's variety show on ABC, which aired on May 8th, attracting a record 41% share of America's TV audience.

Elvis was keen to pursue his career as an actor and was looking forward to more dramatic roles, but unfortunately this wasn't to be the case. Elvis was back in uniform for *G.I.Blues*, which although a box office success, started a formula for another 27 musical films to follow. Producer Hal Wallis stated that "A Presley picture is the only sure thing in Hollywood". This was true, Elvis' movies did extremely well, but after a while all the films seemed too similar, with critics and some fans losing interest.

For publicity reasons, Elvis was always romantically linked with his co-stars, but he had other interests at heart. While serving in the army Elvis met fourteen-year-old Priscilla Beaulieu and eventually persuaded her family to allow Priscilla to move to Graceland in 1963. Elvis and Priscilla married in May 1967 and exactly nine months later, to the day, their daughter Lisa Marie was born.

These were changing times for Elvis. After nearly a decade of movie making he was given a new challenge, when, in June 1968, he taped a television special for NBC. The show, entitled *Elvis*, became known as the *'68 Comeback Special*, which is exactly what it proved to be, a comeback. Back in front of a real audience again, Elvis gave one of the most critically acclaimed performances of his lifetime.

A year later, Elvis returned to Hollywood for the last time. He was ready to move on to greater challenges and put his movie career behind him. In his own words "I got tired of singing to the guys I beat up in the movies."

The world's media were eager to hear of Elvis' plans on his return to
civilian life and a gruelling round of press conferences ensued.
This one was back home in Memphis

The press had already picked up on Elvis' relationship with Priscilla Beaulieu, but he played it down as "no big romance"

The Official Elvis Presley Fan Club Commemorative Album

Taped for ABC on March 26th 1960, Frank Sinatra's Welcome Home
Elvis *attracted a 41% share of America's national TV audience when aired
on May 8th. Elvis is pictured here during rehearsals for the show*

A rare shot of Elvis taken at a Disc Jockey convention in Memphis in 1960

Elvis and Colonel Tom Parker back in business at Graceland

Elvis, back in the army in Paramount's G.I. Blues, Paramount 1960

Elvis as Tulsa MacLean, lead singer in rock'n'roll trio The Three Blazes. Some location work and scenes featuring military manoeuvres were shot while Elvis was still in the Army and in Germany although he did not take part in the filming

May 10th, 1960. Elvis greets King Mahrenda Bir Bikram Shah Deva of Nepal during production of G.I. Blues

There were more royal visitors when three Scandinavian Princesses toured the set

When G.I. Blues *was shown in Mexico, audiences frequently became overexcited and riots ensued, leading to future Presley movies being banned from theatre*

Tulsa (Elvis) and Cooky (Robert Ivers) admiring cabaret singer Lili, played by Juliet Prowse

With co-star Juliet Prowse discussing their next scene with G.I.Blues director, Norman Taurog

Elvis pictured during a break in the recording of the G.I. Blues *soundtrack*

In 20th Century Fox's Flaming Star, *Elvis played a half breed Native American, Pacer Burton*

Flaming Star was
Elvis' sixth movie

*As always, fans flocked
to the set whenever they
were allowed to meet
Elvis during filming*

Elvis and co-star Tuesday Weld in his seventh movie Wild In The Country.
Twentieth Century Fox

Elvis and female co-stars Millie
Perkins and Tuesday Weld in scenes
from Wild In The County

As well as Tuesday Weld, Elvis'
character in Wild in the Country,
Glenn Tyler, enjoyed a romantic
entanglement with Millie Perkins.

*March 1961. Elvis arrives in Hawaii, first to perform a benefit concert
for the U.S.S. Arizona Memorial in Pearl Harbour, then
to begin location filming for* Blue Hawaii

Draping a flower garland, or lei, around the neck of a visitor is a traditional welcome in Hawaii. Elvis almost disappeared under the weight of leis when he arrived in Honolulu

Elvis back in uniform again as Chad Gates in Blue Hawaii, *Paramount 1961*

With co-star Joan Blackman in the grounds of the Cocoa Palms Resort, during production of Blue Hawaii

Director Hal Wallis joins Joan and Elvis for a photo call on the Blue Hawaii *set*

Blue Hawaii *was to become a bigger box office success than any of Elvis' previous films. There was certainly no shortage of fans on hand to support him during filming*

Elvis as reluctant sheriff Toby Kwimper in a scene from Follow That Dream, *United Artists 1961*

Elvis' friend and leading light in the Memphis Mafia, Red West, played a bank guard in Follow That Dream *and is seen here rehearsing a fight scene with Elvis*

Elvis' ninth movie was one of his least remarkable films, although it did produce the hit theme tune EP Follow That Dream

Tough guy actor Charles Bronson looks on as Elvis prepares for his big fight in a scene from Kid Galahad, *United Artists 1962*

Elvis used his martial arts training to the full to give a credible performance as the ex-serviceman turned boxer, Walter Gulick

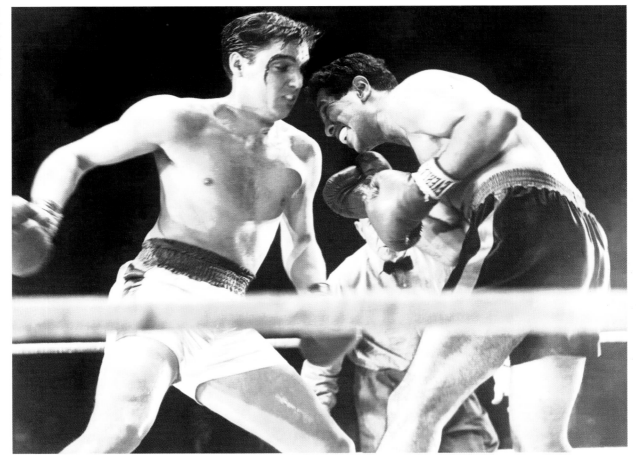

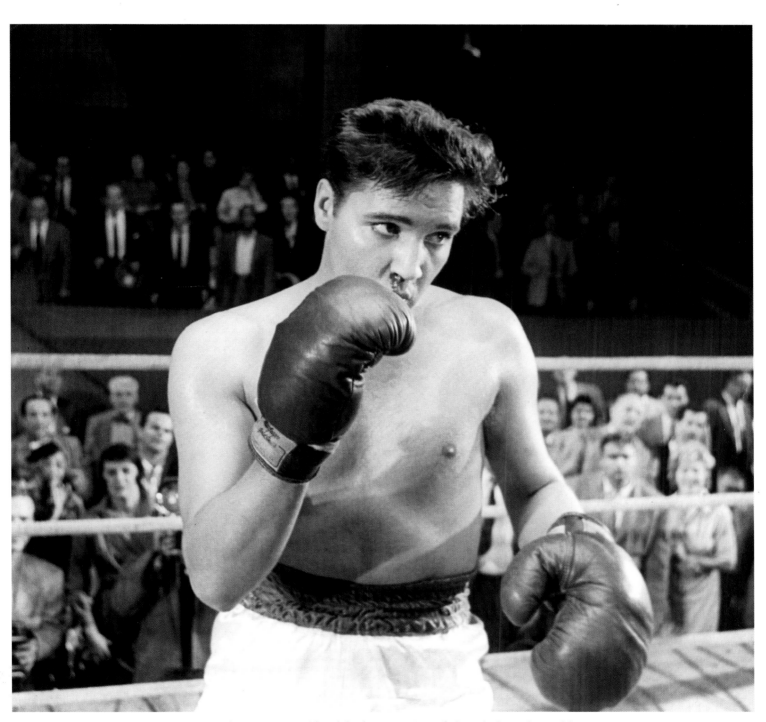

From the six songs in Kid Galahad, *it was* King Of The Whole Wide World
that provided Elvis with yet another hit

Back in Hawaii as sailor Ross Carpenter in Girls! Girls! Girls! *Paramount, 1962*

Elvis' co-star Laurel Goodwin provided the love interest in Girls! Girls! Girls!

Girls! Girls! Girls! was the movie which gave Elvis the international hit single Return To Sender

Elvis hires a young Kurt Russell to kick him in the shins to win
the sympathy of nurse Diane Warren (Joan O'Brien).
It Happened At The World's Fair, *MGM*

Elvis and Gary Lockwood played crop dusting pilots who had fallen on hard times in It Happened At The World's Fair

This rather battered print showing Elvis delighting fans by trying his hand at hairdressing whilst on location for It Happened At The World's Fair *was discovered stuck to a Fan Club application form dating back more than 30 years*

*Mike (Elvis) and Danny
(Gary Lockwood) meet
Sue-Lin played by child
actress Vicky Tiu*

*Mike babby-sitting Sue-Lin at
the Seattle World's Fair*

A year after she had walked out of the water in Dr No, *Bond girl Ursula Andress found herself on a different beach starring opposite Elvis in Paramount's* Fun In Acapulco, *1963*

Elvis played former trapeze artist, part time lifeguard and nightclub singer
Mike Windgren in Fun In Acapulco

The high diving board which causes Mike Windgren such a problem in Fun In Acapulco *doesn't seem quite as daunting in the studio*

In discussion with director Norman Taurog, 1963

Elvis singing Come On Everybody *in his 14th movie*
Viva Las Vegas. *MGM 1964. (Actually released*
after Kissin' Cousins *as his 15th)*

To generate publicity, the movie studios would invariably try to establish romantic links between Elvis and his leading ladies, but the relationship with Ann Margret reportedly went beyond mere speculation

Singing The Lady Loves Me *with Ann Margret*

Elvis and Ann Margret in their unforgettable performance of Come On Everybody

Viva Las Vegas allowed Elvis to indulge his passion for cars as he played Grand Prix driver Lucky Johnson

A double role for Elvis as Josh Morgan and Smokey Mountain Boy Jodie Tatum in Kissin' Cousins, *MGM 1963*

His local roots make 2nd Lieutenant Josh Morgan the ideal choice to liaise with the residents when the Air Force wants to take over part of a Tennessee mountain

The striking resemblance between dark haired Josh Morgan...

...and blond Jodie Tatum leads to the discovery that they are Kissin' Cousins

Elvis' co-star in Roustabout was the highly respected actress Barbara Stanwyck, seen here on the movie set

*Elvis as Charlie Rogers
about to attempt the
Wall of Death*

*As well as being a motor cycle ace, Charlie could, of course, sing, as demonstrated here
during the number* There's A Brand New Day On The Horizon

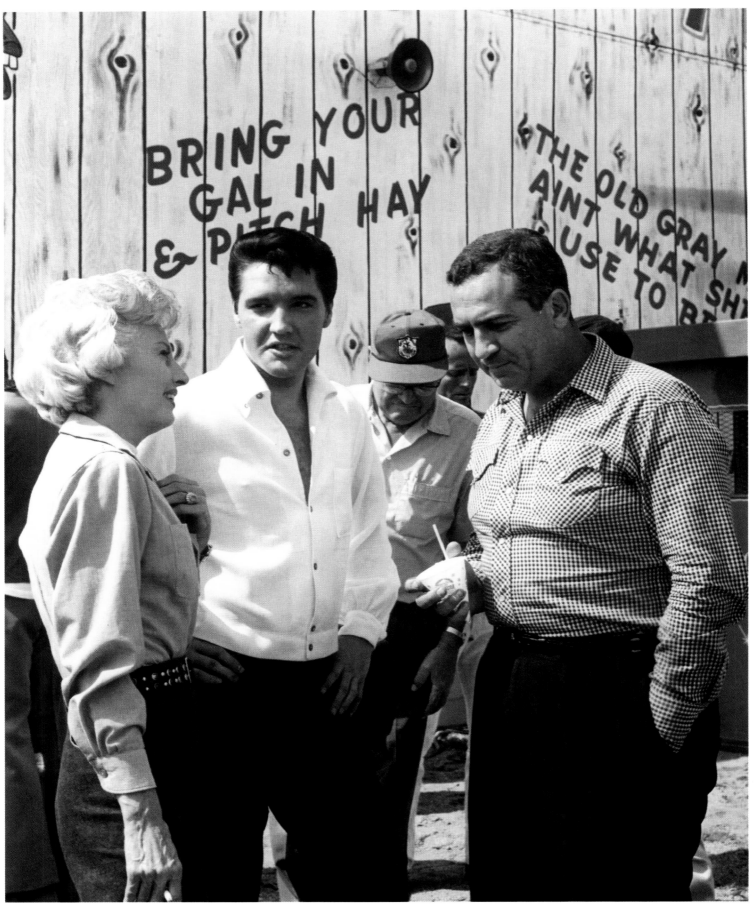

Discussing the next scene on the set of Roustabout

*As well as Barbara Stanwyck, seen here having a little horse trouble, Roustabout's
cast also included a small role as a college student for Raquel Welch*

*British Fan Club Secretary Albert Hand and his wife Phillis met Elvis while
he was filming in November 1961 and he told them, "I loved it in Europe.
I only saw a small part of all I wanted to see whilst I was in the army
over there but one day I shall go back and make up for all the
things I missed the first time around."*

*Rusty Wells (Elvis)
promises to keep an eye on
Big Frank's (Harold J.
Stone) beloved daughter
in MGM's* Girl Happy

*Keeping watch at
the Seadrift Motel,
Fort Lauderdale*

*Elvis performing
the title song,* Girl
Happy *(above)
and* Starting
Tonight *(right)*

Co-star Shelley Fabares joined Elvis as he sang The Meanest Girl In Town

As rodeo star Lonnie Beale, Elvis is hired to help run a health spa ranch in Allied Artists' Tickle Me

Although not really dressed for the part, Elvis helps keep the ladies in trim at the Circle Z ranch

With co-star Julie Adams in Tickle Me

All eyes are on Elvis as he sings Such An Easy Question

Elvis as movie star Johnny Tyrone in an action scene from The Sands of the Desert, *an opening sequence from* Harem Holiday

Another scene from The Sands of The Desert, *the movie Johnny Tyrone is making before he finds himself embroiled in his own desert adventure*

Harem Holiday *was the title given to Elvis' 19th movie for UK release. In America it was known as* Harum Scarum

In an attempt to foil some vicious middle eastern assassins,
Elvis sings Shake That Tambourine

Elvis wins the heart of a young admirer singing Hey Little Girl

*Elvis as Johnny, a riverboat gambler and entertainer,
in United Artists'* Frankie and Johnny

A fortune teller forecasts that Johnny's run of bad luck will change with the arrival of a redhead who duly appears in the shape of Nellie Bly, played by Nancy Kovak

Elvis singing Beginner's Luck *in a scene from* Frankie and Johnny

Elvis' luck at the roulette table certainly seems to be improving until...

...he is accidentally shot by his lover Frankie, played by Donna Douglas

Elvis as helicopter pilot Rick Richards with Donna Butterworth and Marianna Hill in Paramount's Paradise Hawaiian Style

Trying to bring in business for his helicopter charter service, Elvis is persuaded to sing Drums Of The Islands

Donna Butterworth played Jan Kohana, the daughter of Elvis' business partner

During production of Paradise Hawaiian Style, *Elvis vistited the U.S.S. Arizona memorial at Pearl Harbour. His concert at the Broch arena in 1961 helped finance the building of the memorial*

Paradise Hawaiian Style *allowed Elvis to continue his love affair with Hawaii and, although not pictured here, he managed to find a bit part for his friend Red West who was now appearing in his eleventh Elvis movie*

In his next movie, Spinout, *Elvis played racing driver Mike McCoy, who was constantly facing difficult choices – which car to drive, which venue to sing at and which girl to marry*

An open air meal brings a surprise guest
Spinout – MGM 1966

*Elvis with Shelley Fabares
who had previously starred
opposite him in* Girl Happy

Spinout *provided lots of good
opportunities for pool parties*

Spinout *was retitled* California Holiday *for UK release*

English actress Annette Day was Elvis' leading lady in Double Trouble, *MGM 1967*

"You play pretty rough, mister." Elvis as singer Guy Lambert in Double Trouble

In Double Trouble, *Guy Lambert achieved something which Elvis never did by performing at venues in London. Here he is singing* There's So Much World To See

Elvis as navy frogman Ted Jackson in
Easy Come, Easy Go *Paramount, 1967*

Ted Jackson, of course, was a frogman
who could sing and play guitar

In a race to locate a sunken treasure chest Ted needs to take alternative transport as his own car has been remodelled as a work of art

Ted recovers the treasure only to find that it's copper and not gold

Elvis as millionaire Scott Hayward in Clambake, United Artists, 1967

Elvis singing the title song Clambake. Just prior to beginning work on this movie, Elvis purchased the 163 acre Circle G ranch in Mississippi, where he returned once filming was completed

Singing Hey, Hey, Hey *while preparing his boat for a major race*

Elvis with co-star Shelley Fabares (in her third Presley film) in Clambake

May 1st 1967. Elvis and Priscilla were married at a private ceremony at the Aladdin Hotel, Las Vegas. The wedding, which took place at 9.30a.m, was attended by a small group of family and friends

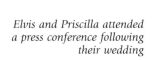

Elvis and Priscilla attended a press conference following their wedding

*After moving to Graceland early in 1963 Priscilla Beaulieu
finally became Mrs Priscilla Presley*

Elvis' co-star in Speedway
was Nancy Sinatra

During production of Speedway *news of Priscilla's pregnancy was released*

Although receiving mixed reviews and lower box office takings, MGM's Stay Away Joe, *still brought in a profit for the studio*

Elvis as Joe Lightcloud in the comedy western Stay Away Joe

Whilst filming Stay Away Joe, *Elvis received this scroll from the International Elvis Presley Appreciation Society*

Proud parents Elvis and Priscilla with Lisa Marie, born February 1st 1968

Elvis on Rising Sun at Graceland in 1968

Meeting fans in Beverly Hills, 1968

If Albert the Great Dane looked like he was enjoying himself in this movie, it may have been because he was Elvis' own dog

Elvis with co-star Michele Carey (Bernice) and Albert in Live A Little, Love A Little. *MGM 1968*

In Live A Little, Love A Little, *Elvis played photographer Greg Nolan*

In June 1968, Elvis gave his first live performance since his Arizona Memorial Benefit in 1961. The show was recorded for the television special Elvis, *now known as the '68 Comeback Special*

With producer Steve Binder during recording of the television special

*Aired on December 3rd 1968 on NBC TV, the Elvis special was one
of the biggest television hits of the year*

At home in front of an audience, Elvis was keen to put Hollywood behind him

*Elvis' performance delighted fans and critics alike, proving that at the age of
33, he was as exciting an entertainer as he had ever been*

*During the show Elvis was joined by his original musicians Scotty Moore
and DJ Fontana for an informal jam session*

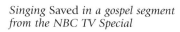

149

The 1960s – "Tired of Singing to the Guys I Beat Up in the Movies"

Back on the big screen in Charro, *a dramatic western where Elvis performed no musical numbers. His only singing role was during the opening credits*

Greeting fans in Beverley Hills during production of Charro *in 1968*

Elvis played outlaw turned lawman Jess Wade in National General's Charro

During production of The Trouble With Girls *Elvis received an award from the
Official Elvis Presley Fan Club of Great Britain in recognition of his support for the
club's fund raising efforts on behalf of Guide Dogs For The Blind*

Elvis in The Trouble With Girls
(And How To Get Into It), *originally
entitled* The Chautauqua

*Baseball personality Duke Snyder meeting Elvis
during production of* The Trouble with Girls

In The Trouble With Girls
*Elvis played showman Walter
Hale who battles to clear his
troupe of a murder charge
and unmasks the true killer*

Spring 1969 on the set of Universal's Change Of Habit

Elvis as Doctor John Carpenter. Change Of Habit *was to be his last movie*

Mary Tyler Moore played opposite Elvis as a nun sent covertly into the community to learn about life

Gospel singer Mahalia Jackson (left) visited the Change Of Habit *set in March 1969 and met Elvis along with another of the film's undercover nuns, actress Barbara McNair*

At the end of the 60s, with his Hollywood days behind him,
Elvis was looking forward to returning to live performances and was about
to move into an entirely new phase of his career

The 1970s

"Every Dream I Have Ever Dreamed has Come True a Hundred Times"

*t*he newly-built International Hotel, Las Vegas, housed the largest showroom in the city and following his successful television special, Elvis was booked for a four-week, fifty seven show engagement. Although originally intended as the opening act for the showroom, the Colonel was keen for Elvis to wait for another act to break in the new venue. Any technical problems associated with the new showroom could, therefore, be cleared up before Elvis appeared. Barbra Streisand was the first act in the showroom, and following her closing night, Elvis opened on July 31st 1969. The show broke all Las Vegas attendance records, bringing acclaim from fans and critics who had travelled from all over the world to see Elvis perform.

Elvis returned to Las Vegas the following year, breaking his own attendance records and following his success in the city, he began to take his show on tour throughout the United States.

In January 1971, Elvis was honoured as 'One of the Ten Outstanding Young Men of the Nation' by the United States Junior Chamber of Commerce. His acceptance speech proved this to be one of the proudest moments of his life.

"When I was a child, ladies and gentlemen, I was a dreamer. I read comic books and I was the hero of the comic book. I saw movies and I was the hero in the movie. So every dream I have ever dreamed has come true a hundred times.

"I'd like to say that I learned very early in life, that without a song, the day would never end. Without a song, a man ain't got a friend. Without a song, the road would never bend.. without a song. So I'll just keep singing the song."

After his triumphant return to the stage in 1969, Elvis gave nearly 1,100 performances, an exhausting tour schedule that contributed to the break up of his marriage (Elvis and Priscilla divorced in October 1973) and put an intolerable strain on his health.

Elvis died at home at Graceland on August 16th, 1977, news that literally shook the world. Aged just 42, in just twenty one years, Elvis had influenced popular culture throughout three decades, and set a precedent for popular music today.

Elvis pictured during the legendary American Sound Recording Sessions in Memphis, January 1969. Hits from this session included In The Ghetto, Suspicious Minds *and* Don't Cry Daddy

Preparing for a triumphant return to the live stage, Elvis visited the site of the new International Hotel in Las Vegas. The hotel was to have the largest showroom in the city and Elvis committed to a four week, 57 show engagement

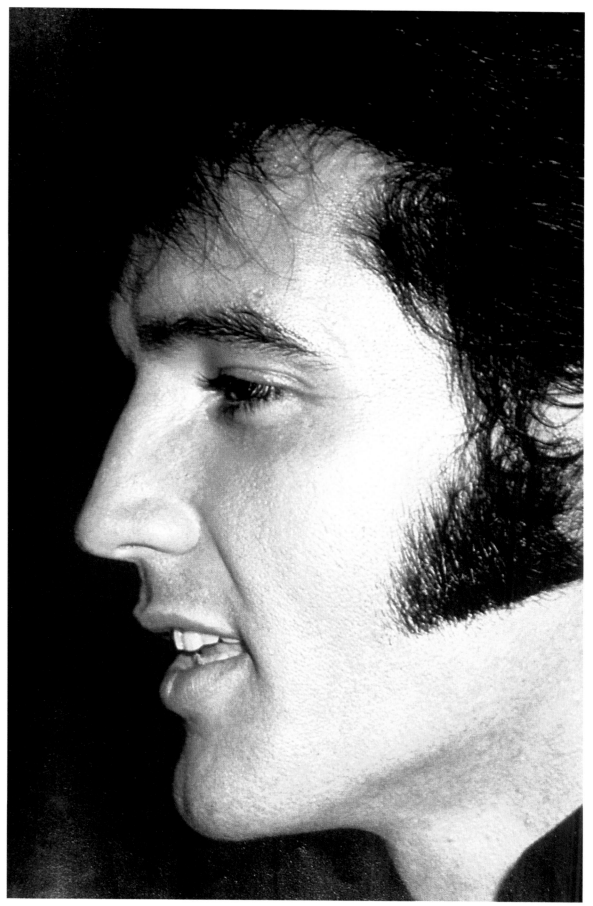

Elvis pictured at a press conference following his opening in Las Vegas

July 31st 1969. Opening night at the International Hotel, Las Vegas, Elvis'
long-awaited return to live performances

*Candid photos from 1969, at home with daughter Lisa Marie
and a shot taken by a fan at the gates to Graceland*

Always appreciating the loyalty of his fans, Elvis took time out to greet them whenever he could – especially the really young ones!

Following an engagement at the Houston Astrodome between Feb 27th and March 1st, Elvis was awarded five gold records at a press conference and is pictured here with RCA Executive Harry Jenkins and RCA President Rocco Laginestra. Elvis' performances at the Astrodome attracted a record 207,494 people

Elvis returned to Las Vegas in January and February 1970 as well as for a summer season in August. MGM were on hand to film his summer festival for the movie That's The Way It Is. *In September Elvis went on a nine-city tour and MGM followed, filming extensively for the movie*

Spring 1970. On Stage at the International Hotel, Las Vegas

*July 1970, in rehearsal. Scenes from these sessions were also
recorded for* That's The Way It Is

August 1970, meeting guests backstage in Las Vegas and sharing a joke
with comedian Sammy Davis Jnr

About to take the stage at the International Hotel.
Guitarist Charlie Hodge is front left

On stage during his summer engagement at the International Hotel

*Elvis' stage wear was designed by Bill Belew. Based on Karate Gis, his
outfits allowed optimum movement on stage*

While in rehearsal at the International Hotel MGM were on hand, filming the documentary That's The Way It Is

Greeting fans on stage in the International Showroom

*On stage during the 1970 Summer
Festival at the International Hotel*

*"Try not to let the lights and cameras throw
you... and try not to throw the lights and
cameras," was a joke often used by Elvis in
the presence of the production crew*

On stage at the International Hotel Las Vegas with his
custom-made Gibson Guitar

*On stage 1970. Many of Elvis' suits were named for reference, mainly by
fans. This suit, known as The Chain Suit, is currently on display in the
Rock'n'Roll Hall of Fame, Cleveland, USA*

Elvis in performance in The Chain Suit, *another Bill Belew's design*

*August 1970. On stage in Las Vegas, Elvis' female backing singers,
The Sweet Inspirations, can be seen seated behind him*

In an attempt to help in the war against illegal drugs, Elvis paid a surprise visit to the White House in Washington in December 1970. President Nixon agreed to meet him and presented him with a Bureau of Narcotics badge, making him an honourary drugs enforcement agent

On January 16th 1971, Elvis was named "One of the Ten Outstanding Young Men of the Nation" by the United States Junior Chamber of Commerce

A family portrait with Priscilla and Lisa Marie

On stage at Hampton Roads, Virginia, April 9th 1972. The tour started in Buffalo on April 5th and he played a different town every night up to Albuquerque on April 19th

On stage in Jacksonville, Florida, April 16th 1972

Following the success of the documentary film That's The Way It Is *MGM return to film a second documentary* Elvis On Tour *during his April tour*

In 1972 during the peak of his concert career. Fans from the UK began to travel with the Fan Club to see Elvis on tour

June 9th 1972. Elvis gave a press conference at the New York Hilton prior to performing four sell-out shows at New York's Madison Square Garden

Elvis pictured at the New York Hilton following his press conference

*In performance at Madison Square Garden. RCA taped the four shows for
the album* Elvis Live at Madison Square Garden

The Madison Square Garden shows were sell-outs, the first time any performer had filled the venue four times consecutively

Elvis went to see Glen Campbell in concert and the two became firm friends

September 5th 1972. Elvis takes part in a press conference announcing Aloha From Hawaii *a television concert to be broadcast globally by satellite*

Elvis arriving in Honolulu on January 9th 1973 to prepare for the
Aloha From Hawaii *television show*

Prior to his live satellite performance, Elvis performed to 6,000 fans in the Honolulu International Center Arena on January 12th. Although technically a dress rehearsal, Elvis gave the same high quality performance as reserved for the live satellite broadcast

*At a second dress rehearsal, the Mayor of Honolulu announced that
January 13th would be Elvis Presley Day*

Elvis pictured in full stage attire for the Aloha From Hawaii *rehearsal.*
During the satellite broadcast Elvis threw his cape into the crowd.
It remained missing until 1995 when it was returned to Elvis' estate

January 14th 1973. Elvis: Aloha from Hawaii – via Satellite *was
broadcast live from the Honolulu International Center Arena beginning
at 12.30am. The show was seen by millions of fans in countries all over
the world. 30 European countries saw the show at a later date and
it was shown in America on April 4th 1973*

In total Elvis: Aloha from Hawaii *was seen in around 40 countries
by up to 1.5 billion people. Its screening in the United States attracted more
than 51% of the viewing audience and was watched by more people
than Neil Armstrong's first steps on the moon*

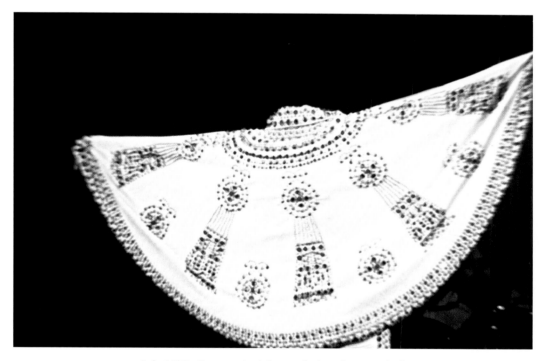

*July 1973. On stage in Atlanta, the last show in which
Elvis wore a cape with his suit*

On tour in 1973 wearing the Orange Starburst Suit. A full programme of touring and engagements saw Elvis performing from February through to September with only a few short breaks in the schedule

Las Vegas, August 1973 with reporter Borje Lundberg and signing a fan's t-shirt

Elvis receiving an N.M.E trophy from British Fan Club Secretary Todd Slaughter.

Elvis first began studying Karate while serving in the army and became a black belt in 1960. He held a great passion for the art, which continued for the rest of his life and is pictured here with Karate champion Ed Parker and Master Kang Rhee, his tutor in Memphis

A rare shot of Elvis in Las Vegas in 1974 wearing a seldom seen white two-piece leather suit

Elvis in 1974 with girlfriend Linda Thompson and associate Jerry Schilling

October 1974 on stage in Dayton, Ohio wearing the Chinese Dragon Suit

October 1974 on stage in Dayton, Ohio wearing the Chinese Dragon Suit

October 1st 1974 introducing singer Kathy Westmoreland during his second night at the Notre Dame Convention Centre in South Bend, Indiana

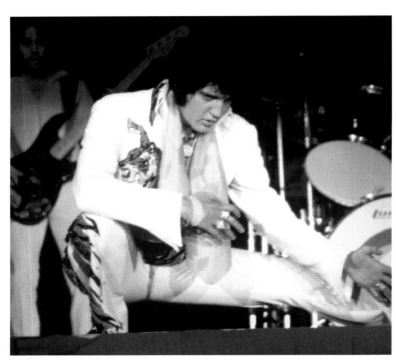

Indianapolis, October 4th 1974 (matinee performance) wearing the Mad Tiger Suit

Elvis on stage during the spring tour of 1975, which featured the rare
appearance of these two piece suits

Elvis on stage in 1975 wearing the Indian Feather Suit

On stage May 31st 1975, during the matinee show in Huntsville, Alabama where Elvis played to over 40,000 people in five shows over three days

On stage May 31st 1975, during the matinee show in Huntsville, Alabama,
midway through the tour which stretched from April 24th to June 10th

On stage May 31st 1975, during an evening show in Huntsville, Alabama

For the May 31st show, Elvis wore one of the many suits
he had decorated with a phoenix design

At the Asheville Civic Center in North Carolina, Elvis wore the Gypsy Suit and is pictured above with his father, Vernon, who had suffered a heart attack earlier in the year

A rare shot of Elvis wearing the Andre Suit

San Diego was included in the spring 1976 tour and Elvis is seen here arriving in his Convair jet, the Lisa Marie, which he had purchased the previous summer

The strangest things were thrown on stage during Elvis' performances including underwear and teddy bears, of course, but also water pistols and, as seen here, shrunken heads and rubber chickens. These shots were taken early in June 1976 in Atlanta where Elvis played four shows in three days. He then had an 18 day break before he was out on the road again

Onstage in Atlanta, wearing one of two designs known as the Bicentennial Suits

December 29th 1976, on stage at the Civic Center, Birmingham, wearing the Gold Inca Leaf Suit

On December 8th 1976, Elvis appeared on stage in Las Vegas for the last time at the Las Vegas Hilton

February 15th 1977, a candid shot taken in a hotel lobby in Montgomery, Alabama

Assisted by Charlie Hodge, Elvis accepts a gift from a fan

*On stage in 1977, wearing the Mexican Sundial Suit, a costume which has
also been called the Aztec or Aztec Calendar Suit*

*June 1977 in Macon, Georgia sitting with
backing group the Stamps Quartet*

*Relaxing on stage alongside
the Sweet Inspirations*

*On May 28, 1977, Elvis played to an audience of nearly
19,000 at the Spectrum in Philadelphia*

*On June 26th 1977 at Indianapolis Airport, Elvis presented an award to
British Fan Club Secretary Todd Slaughter. This photo was taken on the
steps of the Lisa Marie, just hours before his last concert performance*

*Elvis' final concert performance was at the Indianapolis Market Square
Arena, six weeks before his death in August 1977*

Acknowledgments
I would like to acknowledge the following people for their help in this book:
Andrew Hearn, Terry Bellis, Graham Knowles, Andy Wood, Jacen Bruce and
Clare Haynes. Special thanks to Joe Tunzi, Ger Rijff and especially Todd Slaughter,
an inspiration and a great friend.

Picture Credits
Joe Tunzi, J.A.T Productions, PO Box 56372, Chicago, Illinois 60656, USA:
1, 11, 15, 24, 46 (bottom), 39 (bottom right), 41, 42, 46, 55, 66, 67, 73, 82,
138 (bottom), 144, 145, 148, 150, 157, 159, 162, 164, 170, 178, 179, 187, 190,
191, 192, 193, 194, 196, 204 (bottom), 217, 218.
Ger Rijff, Tutti Frutti Productions, Amsterdam: 12, 28, 29, 30, 31, 32, 56 (bottom),
68 (bottom), 69, 80 (top), 161.
London Express News: 22, 58.
Camera Press: 70.
Memories of Elvis (Memphis): 39 (top), 43, 48, 54, 201, 202.
Sean Shaver: 207 (top), 213.
Keith Alverson, PO Box 1666, Palmetto, GA 30268, USA: 197, 202, 203, 204, 205,
206, 207 (bottom), 208 (bottom), 209, 210, 211, 212, 214, 215, 216, 219, 220, 221.